AF344628

Saga of a Lost Soul

Kranthi Veeramachaneni

BookLeaf
Publishing

India | USA | UK

Saga of a Lost Soul © 2024 Kranthi Veeramachaneni

All rights reserved.

No part of this publication may be reproduced, stored in a retrieval system, or transmitted, in any form or by any means, electronic, mechanical, photocopying, recording or otherwise, without the prior written permission of the presenters.

Kranthi Veeramachaneni asserts the moral right to be identified as the author of this work.

Presentation by *BookLeaf Publishing*

Web: www.bookleafpub.com

E-mail: info@bookleafpub.com

ISBN: 9789360940034

First edition 2024

This book is dedicated to all the Souls-Keepers who wander in the shadows, seeking light, solace, and connection in a world that often feels unfamiliar and unforgiving. May these words serve as a reminder that in moments of darkness, there is always a glimmer of hope waiting to be discovered.

With love and solidarity,

KV

ACKNOWLEDGEMENT

In the moments of creating this collection, I am humbled and grateful for the unwavering inspiration that have intricately woven themselves into every verse and word. To those whose presence has illuminated my path and whose voices have echoed in the silent spaces between lines, I extend my heartfelt gratitude.

PREFACE

Each piece within these pages is a fragment of
my soul, a whisper from the depths of my being
searching for connection and understanding.
Through the rhythm of verse and the power of
prose, I have attempted to capture the fleeting
moments of clarity, the tangled emotions, and
the timeless struggles that shape our existence.

I invite you to walk alongside me through the
corridors of vulnerability. With each turn of the
page, may you discover a reflection of your own
innermost thoughts and feelings, and may you
find comfort in the knowledge that you are not
alone in your quest for meaning, connection, and
the profound beauty of the human spirit.

Thank you for joining me on this odyssey of the
soul. Together, let us navigate the labyrinth of
emotions, embrace the shadows of our past, and
ultimately, emerge into the light of
understanding.

With heartfelt gratitude,
KV.

VILOHIT

In the cosmic dance of celestial grace, emerges a
divine embrace.
With ash smeared on his radiant skin,
a symbol of life's cycle, where new begins.

TWIN SOUL

Encountered a soul, pure
As a child seeking a firm grip.
As a flower's thirst for a nurturer.
As a lion's pride and deep as a sea.
She encountered a soul, as
A reflection of her in a mirror
Craving for life's devotion and
In the midst of the thought storm,
She realised she was in love.
With her twin soul.

Embrace

After a day so long and grey,
Beneath burdens heavy
and thoughts astray,
a sanctuary so divine,
Where shadows merge into sunshine,
I find my way to your embrace,
Where all my worries start to erase.

A momentary blissful vacation,
In that hug, a silent conversation.
In this silent language,
We rise, we soar above.
Each heartbeat, be it a last beat,
I find my pace to your embrace,
into peace,
To cherish the quiet space,
with sacred grace.

Word

"In the complexity of human communication, every word and gesture weaves a nuanced situation, perceived through the limits of the receiver's mind.

Yet, in the pursuit of peace, genuine communication becomes the untangling hand, unravelling every intricately woven thread."

Rhythm

Ebbs and flows,
In both love and moon phases,
life's mysteries abound.
A testament to endurance,
through time's relentless test,
In the moon's eternal cycle,
Love finds its rest.

Voyage

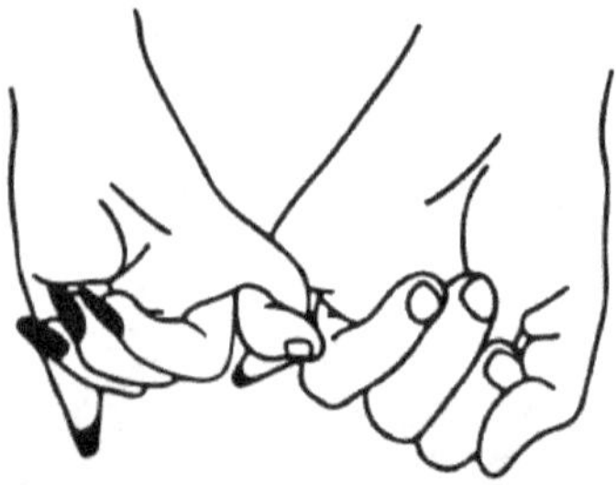

She, a flame burning bright and wild,
He, a calm river, gentle and mild.
Their love, a tempest of heat and cold.
She scorched his depths with her fiery gaze,
He quenched her flames with a gentle haze.

But as they danced in this delicate trance,
Their differences led to a painful chance.
a clash they couldn't tame,
And so, their love drowned in sorrow's claim.

In a world where fire meets water's embrace,
A tale of love doomed to a sombre place.

Now she's left to flicker, alone in the night,
He drifts away, lost in the river's might.
Their love, a story of elements in strife,
Left broken and scattered, in the depths of life.

Prime

Emotions, a palette rich and vast,
In every soul, quietly revealing.

Joy, dances like sunlight on the sea,
It's the laughter that echoes in the air,
A reminder of the moments we share.

Sorrow, a shadow, soft and deep,
wraps us in its gentle, dark embrace,
Teaching strength, as we find our grace.

Fear, a storm that rages wild,
Yet, in its grip, we find our might,
Turning darkness into guiding light.

Anger, a fire that burns within,
from its ashes, wisdom to rise,
A phoenix of understanding in disguise.

Love, the thread that binds them all,
In its embrace, we rise and fall.
A force so gentle, yet mighty and grand,
It holds us together, hand in hand.

Emotions, a palette rich and vast,
In every soul, weave and sew.

Eternal

Hey Krishna, from yesterday to today,
and tomorrow anew,
who shall call your name?
In this eternal, ever-changing game.

Yesterday it was someone,
Today it's my turn beneath the sun,
under the vast blue,
Speaking words, heartfelt and true.

Tomorrow, who will voice their plea?
Under the same sapphire sea.

Hey Krishna, in this dance of voices, crafted with love,
each voice echoes true,
through time's swift river, ever slow.

Unison

Two hearts whisper secrets in the night,
In the quiet fold of an embrace, so tight,
Creating a rhythm, love's to keep,
Beating in concert, soft and deep.

Under the sweep of a subtle moon,
Bound by the serenade of a tender tune.
Each pulse a whisper of desires told,
In the hug where hearts boldly hold.

Two hearts in harmony, soft and clear,
A perfect melody for only them to hear.
In this embrace, their worlds entwine,
Beating in unison, they become one.

Haze

In the theatre of whispers, assumptions take the stage,
a silent play, where truth can disengage.
Conclusions drawn with a hasty pen,
in the margins of understanding, assumptions begin.

A fleeting glance, a misunderstood word,
Assumptions echo, sometimes unheard.
Yet, let's unravel the veils we contrive,
Question assumptions, the truths they deceive.

For in the realm of assumptions' haze,
Misunderstandings find their maze.
Peel back the layers, unveil the core,
In the garden of clarity, assumptions no more.

Naive

Ignorance's dance, a joyful tune,
In its caress, under the blissful moon.
No weight of knowing,
just pure delight,
In the garden of naivety,
everything's bright.

Revive

A soul left in the dirt.

I tried to grasp your elusive rhyme,
To understand you, into the depths,
where emotions wend,
yet shattered, unable to mend.

I gave it all, though it felt tender.
Reaching out to mend, to comprehend,
But at the end, broken, unable to transcend.

I offered all, though it hurt,
my heart extended, yet broken to a point, forever
unintended.

A soul left in the dirt.

Artistry

In a world where hearts beat as one,
Is being sensitive truly undone?

A soul that feels, a heart that weeps,
In emotions' depth, to feel deeply is a gift,
not a flaw.

To be moved by a sunset's gentle hue,
Or feel a friend's joy, so pure and true.

Yet whispers linger, a subtle song,
Questioning if sensitivity is wrong.

In the melody of emotions, a canvas painted with
life's intricate awe,
being sensitive is where,
the soul grows strong.

The Guru

In these times of knowledge's vast sea,
Where wisdom's bullets freely flee,
Quoting alone is not the key, you see.

Beyond the quotes that grace the air,
Lies understanding, deep and rare,
To analyse in every glare,
And implement, with utmost care.

Guru's essence, a shining light,
Not just in words, but insight,
Teaching not to merely recite,
But to live the truth, day and night.

Preaching not as a distant sage,
But walking with you, every stage,
In life's intricate, endless page,
A mentor, wise, in every age.

wabi-sabi

How long!?

When you are broken, several times or more,
A phoenix emerges from the heart's core.
In fragments, you find strength anew,
Each shattered piece, resilience grew?

How long!?

Through the cracks, the light seeps in,
A mosaic of scars, where does healing begin?
For in the brokenness, each fracture tells of
a battle
of lessons learned, and growth sought.

How long!?

Each shattered piece, the mosaic of scars,
a testament true,
to the strength that resides in you.
Resilience grew?

Veil

A puppeteer's dance, subtle and sly,
Strings pulled, truths made to comply.

Whispers of influence, a web tightly spun,
Illusions created, the game's begun.

Behind a mask, motives concealed,
In the guise of trust, truths are revealed.

A chessboard of minds, strategic and cold,
navigate wisely, see through the charade,

In the dance of manipulation,
let authenticity cascade.

Miraa

She is not your first choice,
maybe she wishes to be your last...

Her life is yours.
May be not this,
Previous and the next...

Admire

Quiet in the darkness of the night,
Where thoughts blend with the shadows tight.

In the depths of introspective gaze,
Beauty hidden in an introvert's space.

Not confined but uniquely composed,
A secret realm where silence is disclosed.

Without self, yet wonderfully defined,
In quiet whispers, admiration is entwined.

Envy

In shadows deep where green eyes gleam,
Envy dances, a silent, wicked dream.
Casting tendrils,
a venomous gaze.
It knits a tale of discontent's maze.
A poison that seeps,
a corrosive art,
Envy thrives, tearing friendships apart.

Integrity

In these auspicious times, let's read a story from history…

Once upon a time, there was a prince and a king, from far, far away states.

Prince, extremely handsome, vigorous yet truthful, virtuous, adept yet grounded, handled his power with gratitude and grace. He won his subjects' and a princess's hearts with his devotion and integrity. He never lost his qualities, nor was he blamed for losing his precious years and power for envious requests. He never angered nor devoured his righteous path, even when he was forced to leave his love.
With his equal respect for all beings and his principled life, even gods were feared.

Eventually, after a great walk through his low times, he was wished by all to be a king, where his rule became a benchmark.

And there's the mighty king, the greatest devotee of Hara. A great scholar, a capable ruler, a maestro of the Veena, a master of the sciences, and an able leader.

The mind-born child of the creator, himself, bestowed an indestructible boon.

He had everything: a great kingdom, talented siblings, a beautiful family, unmatched knowledge, and strength.

But with all this might, he felt almighty and became the personification of lust. Lust is about selfishness, greed, ego, and arrogance.

The day he completely became a slave to his senses and couldn't control his desires, he not only destroyed himself and his clan, but the whole kingdom was reduced to ashes. Having all this knowledge but not being able to harness his powers was one of his biggest regrets as he lay dying on the battlefield. He regretted not practising the wisdom he had in his life, which eventually led to his downfall.

Moral of the story: (Readers can conclude)

win?

Even the Sun is clouded twice a day…
Argue or agree,

Does the Sun lose his throne?
Don't the Clouds win twice a day?
Is it the play of Time?

Even the Sun is clouded twice a day…
Argue or agree.

yet..

She, a happy child
Life-affirming…
a happy child, but
as a darker twist to every story,
ruined by air around.

She, a happy warrior
conflicts with yin and yan of thoughts..
a happy child, yet
stands tough to win-or-bust.

Paint

Imagine a barren land.

Seasons fly
Strangers pass
neither a mist nor a drizzle
The last few leaves look up to the sky with hope.

Seasons fly
The last leaf breathes a scent of petrichor.
Trust in hope arises.
A drop here, a drizzle there
giggles with love- love for life.

Suddenly, harsh beams of light explode.
Life dies
The last leaf of trust falls.
Strangers pass, and seasons fly.

Imagine a barren land.

Just

Every spark has a start and an end.
Every breath has to unite with the creator.
Actuality is to embrace both equally.

The Greatest Battle

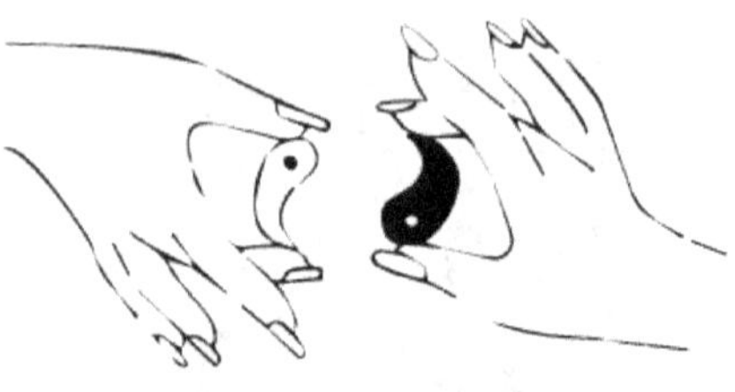

ever deserving yet wondered
ever natural yet catastrophic
ever excruciating yet amusing
is between the heart and the mind.

CHISEL

In the shadows where intentions bend,
Manipulation weaves a deceptive blend.

A puppeteer's dance, subtle and sly,
Strings pulled, truths made to comply.

Whispers of influence, a web tightly spun,
Illusions created, the game's begun.

Crafty words, a masterful art,
Manipulation's dance, tearing apart.

Behind a mask, motives concealed,
In the guise of trust, truths are revealed.

A chessboard of minds, strategic and cold,
Manipulation's tale, often untold.

Beware the puppeteer, hidden in plain sight,
For manipulation thrives in the absence of light.

Yet, in awareness and clarity's embrace,
The puppet's strings can find release.

In the labyrinth of manipulation's deceit,
A sovereign mind may find its beat.

So, navigate wisely, see through the charade,
In the dance of manipulation, let authenticity cascade.

SNOG

Let a kiss on the temple's vein,
take away the day's strain.

Let a hug unite our hearts,
in the symphony of their beats.

Let my deep breath,
tickle your neck.

Let my last beat,
forever be your first.

IGNITE

A poetic enchantress
ignites, breaking chains of conformity,
as new horizons excite.
A march of ideas, where
The seeds of progress grow.
A poetic enchantress
ignites.

VOID

A poignant, exquisite pain, so deep,
crafting both enchanting dreams
and haunting screams.
A cry for the one who isn't near.

It carves out a hollow deep in my core.
A void that throbs until we meet once more.
But in this pain, there is also light,
so deeply might be our plight.

For every tear that love elicits,
Is proof of the depth of its exquisite visits.
For all the art that we still have to make,
I endure this loving ache.

Phantom

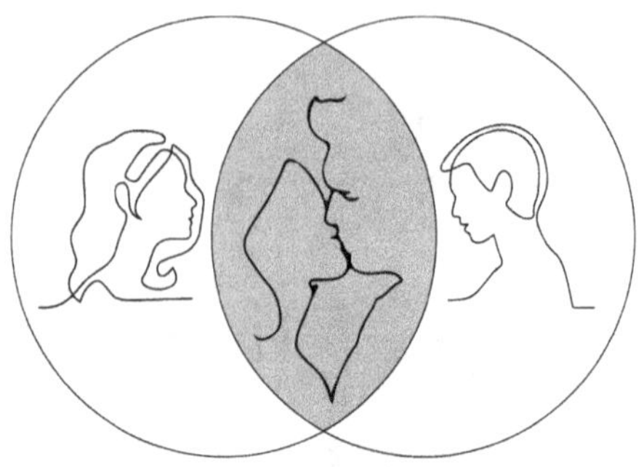

Whispers of past in the night air,
Echoes of times when life was fair,
Now shadows dance where light once played,
A silent waltz in twilight's shade.

Eyes that once sparked with endless fire,
Now hold the weight of lost desire,
A spirit searching, yearning still,
For pieces, time can never fill.

She roams through fields of memory,
A phantom of what used to be,
In every step, a silent plea,
For solace in her misery.

For even in the darkest night,
The soul that's lost can find its light,
In every tear, in every sigh,
There lives a spark that cannot die.

Farewell

Paths diverge, in the dance of fate,
Yet, in our hearts, the bond remains great.

Through the drapes of moments, we've spun,
A chapter concludes, a new one begins.

Farewell, not an end, but a passage in the time,
In the symphony of life, we'll find a common home.